National Learning Association
Everything You
Should Know About:
BASILISK LIZARDS
Faster Learning Facts

By: Anne Richards

INTRODUCTION

Basilisk lizards are some of the most fascinating reptiles on the planet. Not only can these reptiles swim, climb, and hunt like other reptiles can, they also have a few incredible abilities that are all their own. Some Basilisk lizards are found throughout tropical regions in Central America, while others can be seen at your local zoo. They have been featured in popular culture, and have been compared to figures both ancient as well as current for their incredible talents. Do you really think it's possible for a lizard to walk on water? If you want to find out, you'll just have to keep reading!

WHAT DO THEY LOOK LIKE?

Basilisk lizards are types of lizards that have a unique look that makes them easy to tell apart from other kinds of lizards. Their scaly skin is usually green in color, with variations from greenish-brown to olive-green scales on their topside, with white stripes that run from their mouths down along the sides of their necks. They also have large crests that run down their backs, making Basilisk lizards look like miniature pelycosaurs, which were ancient dinosaurs that had large crests on their backs as well. These features make identifying Basilisk lizards in the wild or at the zoo pretty easy.

BASILISK LIZARDS IN MYTHOLOGY

Basilisk lizards didn't just get their names because some scientist somewhere decided to make one up. The name of these amazing creatures actually comes from Greek mythology. In old Greek legends, a basilisk was actually a formidable reptile, considered to be the king of all reptiles on earth. It was said that this reptile king was so powerful, that it could destroy all of its enemies with just a look from its piercing eyes. The Basilisk lizards that we know of today don't have these kinds of powers, but the ability to walk on water is a pretty good substitute for the supernatural abilities of the mythical Greek beast.

WHERE CAN THEY BE FOUND?

The varying range of Basilisk lizards is very small compared to the range of many other common lizards, like the house lizards that we see scurrying about almost every spring. Basilisk lizards can be found in the wild in the tropical rainforests of Central America, from the southern tip of Mexico to the country of Panama. Their limited range is mainly due to their very specific needs with regards to living environment. The tropical climate, humidity, and various water sources make Central America a perfect locale for these water-walking lizards.

THEY BELONG TO THE ORDER SQUAMATA

The families of Basilisk lizards, both close as well as extended, are rather huge. The order that these lizards belong to is called Squamata. This order comprises all of the lizards and snakes in the world. It is also the third largest order of vertebrates that are alive today. The suborder that Basilisk lizards belong to is called Iguana, which you've probably heard of before. This means that Basilisk lizards are closely related to iguanas (of course), chameleons, anoles, and agamids which are all lizards that bare some similarities to Basilisk lizards. Unlike Basilisk lizards, though, none of these lizard cousins can walk on water.

WHAT'S SPECIAL ABOUT THEIR FEET?

Most lizards have feet that get them around pretty well on land, but did you know that the feet Basilisk lizards have can get them around on water, too? That's because Basilisk lizards have really long toes on their posterior feet. These toes have flaps of skin that are usually hidden between the toes when the lizards are on land. If something happens that causes these lizards to make a break for the water, these

flaps, or fringes, will actually open up so that th
lizards can run across the water! The feet of Basilis
lizards serve a pretty cool purpose.

HOW BIG ARE THEY?

Basilisk lizards, while not huge reptiles, are larger than many of their reptilian cousins. The average size for an adult Basilisk lizard is anywhere from two to two-and-a-half feet in length, including the tail. They can also weigh up to seven ounces, or about two hundred grams. The female Basilisk lizards are about half of the size of the male lizards, making them rather easy to tell apart. Don't go thinking these creatures are that big, though; the tails of Basilisk lizards make up about three-quarters of their total body length, making these lizards a whole lot of tail.

THEY COME IN A VARIETY
OF COLORS

Like many other types of lizards, Basilisk lizards come in a variety of greens. The color green is one of the most common colors for many lizards to have, mainly because it helps the lizards match up with their environments. The Basilisk lizards are no different, and depend on their variations of brownish-green to olive-green colors to help them blend in with their surroundings. Their varying colors work like camouflage, making it hard for their predators to see them whether they are in the tree canopies and surrounded by leaves or crawling around on the forest floor.

WHERE DO THEY LIVE?

The habitat of Basilisk lizards is a relatively small one. These lizards are not as adaptable to different habitats as other lizards are, so their homes are in rather specific areas of the world. Basilisk lizards prefer to live in tropical areas, where the humidity is high and the heat can easily reach the triple digits in the daytime. Green Basilisk lizards spend a lot of their time living in trees and hanging out on the branches and limbs of the thick forest canopies.

Basilisk lizards also make it a point to never stray to far away from a water source. Not only is wate necessary for their dietary survival, it's also convenient escape route should a predator come alon and pose a threat.

CAN THEY REALLY SWIM?

Basilisk lizards are more widely known for their ability to run across the surface of the water, an incredible display of both speed and agility. But did you know that these lizards are accomplished swimmers, too? Basilisk lizards are excellent swimmers, and even have the capability of holding their breath for almost thirty minutes. This is important because these lizards can only run across the top of the water for about fifteen feet before sinking, meaning that they have to depend on their ability to swim at one point or another. Luckily this isn't a problem for this agile creature.

THEY CAN RUN ON THE SURFACE OF THE WATER, TOO!

The most amazing ability that Basilisk lizards exhibit is their ability to run across the surface of the water to escape potential threats and predators. This wild talent sets Basilisk lizards apart from every other lizard, or animarl rather, in the world. This incredible feat is accomplished when these lizards utilize the wide flaps of skin that are located in between their toes. These flaps actually increase the surface area of their feet. They rapidly slap the water as they run which makes a small air cushion between their feet and the top of the water that prevents them from sinking. Quite an amazing ability indeed.

HOW DO THEY REPRODUCE?

The reproductive habits of Basilisk lizards are similar to other members of the lizard family. These lizards mate sexually, with the male lizards spending time during the mating season looking for a proper mate by impressing the female lizards with their crests. After mating has occurred, the female Basilisk lizards will dig a shallow hole into the ground, where they will then lay anywhere from twelve to eighteen eggs. After the females cover the eggs back up with soil, they leave the area. When properly covered an incubated, the eggs hatch in eight to ten weeks.

TELL ME ABOUT THEIR MATING RITUALS

Many reptiles have different ways of finding mates of the opposite sex for reproduction, and Basilisk lizards are no different. Both male and female Basilisk lizards have crests on their backs that increase in height with age, but only the male lizards have high crests on their heads and tails, too. These high crests are used to impress female Basilisk lizards. The higher the crest of a male, the more likely that lizard is to find a suitable female companion. This just goes to show that female Basilisk lizards really do believe that looks are all that matters.

WHAT TYPES OF FOOD DO THEY LIKE TO EAT?

The diet of Basilisk lizards is rather diverse. Basilisk lizards are omnivores, meaning that they are meat eaters as well as plant eaters. This allows Basilisk lizards to be very opportunist eaters, which just means that they can eat whatever they can get their claws on! Basilisk lizards eat all types of small insects, including ants, beetles, and arthropods. They're also known to eat small vertebrates from time to time.

When they're not in the mood for meat, Basilis
lizards will search out plants, fruits, and berries to ea
There's always a wide variety of food on the menu fc
Basilisk lizards!

HOW DO THEY HUNT
FOR THEIR PREY?

Like many other types of lizards, Basilisk lizards are considered omnivores, which means that they survive on a diet of both plants and animals. They are known to stalk their animal prey slowly before attacking. Sometimes they even lay in wait, remaining as still as possible so insects or even small vertebrates that are passing by don't take notice of them, until it's too late. When they are not hunting, Basilisk lizards

spend the time they are not going after moving pre
searching for stationary food, like plants, berries, an
fruits.

DO THEY HAVE A LOT OF PREDATORS?

Basilisk lizards are rather large compared to other lizards in their family, but are still small enough to be prey for many other creatures in the wild. There is no lack of predators that would love to make a meal out of the Basilisk lizard. Animals that these lizards have to look out for include birds, snakes, and even some mammals. The most common reaction these lizards have when trying to escape a predator is to run to the

closest water source and take off across the surface
but because some large fish will eat these lizards as
well, they try their best to limit their time in the water

WHY DO BASILISK LIZARDS LIKE TO BASK IN THE SUN?

The behavior of Basilisk lizards is generally very similar to that of other members of the lizard family. All lizards are considered ectothermic, which means that they do not have the ability to fully control their body temperature from inside of their bodies. That is why lizards are considered cold-blooded, and why they rely so much on external heat to keep them warm. Basilisk lizards are no different, and when they

are not hunting or looking for plants to eat, they ca
oftentimes be seen lying in the sunlight. This is
common practice for Basilisk lizards so that they ca
warm their cold-blooded bodies.

HOW LONG DO THEY LIVE?

The lifespan of Basilisk lizards varies greatly. The threats that these lizards face in the wild make it difficult to put specific numbers on their longevity, but most scientists agree that they can live in the wild anywhere from five to ten years. Many Basilisk lizards have lived up to ten years in captivity, which most likely denotes their maximum lifespan, considering that they receive the best care and treatment while under the guardianship of the very people that study them. Even though their lifespan are short compared to humans, they are actually rather long compared to many other types of smaller lizard that only live a few years.

MANY BASILISK LIZARDS
CAN BE FOUND
IN FLORIDA

Even though the natural habitat of Basilisk lizards is in a relatively small portion of Central America, many Basilisk lizards have taken up residence in a new place, at the southern tip of the United States: Florida. Basilisk lizards are not indigenous, or naturally-occurring, in the state of Florida, but the exotic pet trade over the course of several years has led to a influx of these water-walking creatures dwellin throughout the entire southern portion of the state Many times people will buy these lizards as pets onl to release them when they get tired of taking care o them. The lizards eventually start to reproduce in th wild, creating what is called a feral population o Basilisk lizards living abroad.

WHY ARE THEY CALLED JESUS CHRIST LIZARDS?

Basilisk lizards get their primary name from Greek mythology, but did you know that some people have given these lizards a Christian nickname? Another name that Basilisk lizards go by is "Jesus Christ lizards," after the man that was the basis for the founding of modern-day Christianity, Jesus Christ. One of the stories that can be found in the New Testament of the Christian Holy Bible involves Jesus walking on water during a violent storm on the Sea of Galilee. This is a very popular bible story, and any Christian that was witnessing Basilisk lizard "walking on water" would probably think back to what they learned about Jesus in Sunday school.

Thank you! Thank you! Thank you!

It means a lot to us that you chose our book to spend your time learning with - we hope you enjoyed it!

All pictures and words were put together, with love, by experts from around the globe. Experts who love what they do and want to improve and educate the world, one book at a time!

We would really appreciate it if you could PLEASE take a second to let us know how we're doing by leaving a review on Amazon.

To leave feedback, Simply visit:

US Customers: https://amazon.com/feedback
UK Customers: https://amazon.co.uk/feedback

For all other customers, you can visit the "Your Orders" link from your Amazon menu and choose "Leave Seller Feedback".

Any comments you may have - what you enjoyed, any suggestions you might have and what you would like to read about in future books.

Any comments will help us understand better what you and your children most enjoy - this allows us to tailor future books and provide exactly what is most helpful and useful in the future.

National Learning Association

CPSIA information can be obtained
at www.ICGtesting.com
Printed in the USA
BVHW021456010419
544248BV00006BB/39/P